Copyright © 2021 Shannon Guerra

With gratitude to the contributing authors, who each retain the copyright for their individual works.

All rights reserved. No part of this book may be reproduced in any form or by any electronic or mechanical means, including information storage and retrieval systems, without permission in writing from the publisher, except by reviewers, who may quote brief passages in a review.

ISBN 978-1-7360844-3-4

Published by Copperlight Wood
P.O. Box 870697
Wasilla, AK
99687
www.copperlightwood.com

Design by Shannon Guerra. Photography by Shannon Guerra, with the exception of pages 31-33 by Cynthia Hellman (desert photos), 44-47 by Jessica Dassow, 54-55 by Renee Petty, and 63 by Megan Ancheta.

Unless noted otherwise, scripture quotations are from the ESV® Bible (The Holy Bible, English Standard Version®), copyright © 2001 by Crossway, a publishing ministry of Good News Publishers. Used by permission. All rights reserved.

Portions of scripture in **bold** are the author's emphasis.

This title may be purchased in bulk for ministry or group study use. For more information, please email shop@copperlightwood.com.

Printed and bound in the USA.

contributors

MĒGAN ANCHETA

Kodiak kid, yarn snob,
owner of Allergy Free Alaska, LLC
www.allergyfreealaska.com
allergyfreealaska@gmail.com

ROBIN ANGAIAK

wannabe book nerd, amateur naturalist,
raising her tribe of six in Alaska

JESSICA DASSOW

wrangler of many boys and a princess,
drinker of unintentionally cold tea,
seeker of sand & sunshine
www.planted-by-the-river.com

CYNTHIA HELLMAN

chocolate snob, drummer, laundry avoider
www.cultivatedgraftings.blogspot.com

RENEE PETTY

third generation Alaskan, singer of songs,
pursuer of healing, superstar auntie

contents

06
come hungry

11
we know Who brings the fire

16
when the dust settles

20
winning the battle

24
be like the bird

25
unexpected terrain

31
rooted in hope

34
how we hold our ground

38 shining through

43 hope is the thing with feathers

44 waiting for home

48 hope is a weapon

50 budding

54 whispered hope

56 hashbrowns & jalapeño aioli

60 bakery style double chocolate muffins

63 what leads to victory

69 philippians 1:9-11

70 study guide

75 notes

come hungry

It's a question Vince and I answer about seventy times a week. Considering that only five of our kids are fully verbal and a week has only so many days, that means that half the time, these guys aren't even paying attention to the answer.

It goes like this:

A kid meanders into the kitchen, and asks the big question: "What's for dinner?"

The first couple of times they ask, I don't mind. So I tell him it's spaghetti.

"Oh." He leaves, and another kid comes to the kitchen. Asks the same thing, gets the same answer. Exits stage right.

A minute goes by, and someone else comes in. Or maybe it's the first kid who already forgot what I told him. Either way, I can already see where this is going.

"What's for –"

"See if you can figure it out."

The kid looks around for clues. A package of pasta on the counter, a red sauce bubbling on the back of the stove.

"Uh...spaghetti?"

"We have a winner! Yes."

A few more minutes go by. Our six-year-old comes in.

"What's for dinner?"

"Go look."

She goes to the stove, lifts the lid off the pot on the front burner. Peeks in, drops the lid, turns around, and cries, "We're having *hot water* for *dinner*?!"

That girl is full of surprises.

But I think I know how she feels. I'm also the little girl running to the storehouse, asking her Father, "What are we doing now?" And I expect an exciting answer – something fun, or at least interesting.

He tells me to look and see for myself, but what's right in front of me is not what I was hoping for: Laundry and dishes. Consequences and discipline. Bills and diagnoses. And it feels like we're having hot water for dinner.

Sure, He's got other things cooking on other burners and there are all sorts of preparations happening on the countertop – but we look into this pot right in front of us, and all we see is hot water.

Mamas, I know your work is exhausting. I'm right there with you.

Wives, I know the man you're married to can be a real piece of work sometimes. I know it because, if we're honest, we can be a real piece of work sometimes, too.

Pastors and leaders, I know your team and your congregation don't always appreciate you like they should. Many of you are going for it with all you've got while others are happy to take you for all you have – and sometimes it feels like there's just not much left, anyway. Just hot water.

We look at our immediate circumstances and see nothing of significance. We're hungry for that thing we've been working toward and longing for – the job, the relationship, the healing, the conviction, the decision. It is beyond us and seems so out of reach. We want to go from glory to glory, not paycheck to paycheck. We want to look for victory, but if we're honest, we're really just waiting for the next shoe to drop.

Once when we were in the waiting, our little girl needed therapy to the tune of several thousand dollars and our insurance didn't cover it. We gave the enemy the virtual middle finger and trusted God to do His best, but it felt like hot water.

But when we think about it, a year ago, or two years ago, we were all in a different place, weren't we? Some of us moved, or got a new job, or took on some major life change. And things haven't worked out exactly like we thought they would.

And God says, *Hey Love, sometimes you'll get challenges that you didn't think you signed up for. But I'll also give you gifts that you didn't think to ask for.*

> *As they go through the Valley of Baca [weeping]*
>   *they make it a place of springs;*
>   *the early rain also covers it with pools.*
> *They go from strength to strength;*
>   *each one appears before God in Zion.*
> - Psalm 84:6-7

This isn't where I thought we would be now, either. Not long ago, our youngest was just a speck in God's eye and we didn't even know he existed. God has done things for each of us that were beyond us, beyond our asking.

And I'm still doing, He says.

We miss the ingredients at play all around us, and ask, "We're having hot water for dinner?" As in, *This is all you've got for us? That's it? This is the big breakthrough we've been waiting for?*

We brush over the details like a six year old who only notices what is right in front of her nose, but misses all the preparations on the counter and what is already cooking on the back burner.

No, Love, He says. Stop your panicking. I'm making one of your favorites.

He's full of surprises, too. May we be brave enough to anticipate a feast.

we know Who brings the fire

One night, all of the following played out in our house in the span of just twenty minutes during dinner prep:

I was blending mashed potatoes in the KitchenAid (do you do this, too?) and the bowl looked recklessly full. Vince saw trouble ahead and asked, "Want me to get the splash guard?" right as I flipped the switch on. Before I could answer, chunks of potato flew out at both of us.

This was right after I grabbed a jar of chicken broth from the fridge to make gravy with – and friends, it's important to listen to those promptings of the Holy Spirit, because in case you didn't know, I have almost no sense of smell. So I tasted the contents of the jar first and immediately switched it out, because I almost made gravy out of kombucha.

Amid those distractions we found our toddler in the baking cabinet, covered in flour. And while we (by "we" I mean Vince, of course; I was still cleaning potatoes) brushed him off, Afton asked, "Cham, would you be mad if I—"

"Yes," she answered. And we'll never know what he was hoping to do.

And then another child had *finally* finished school for the day and he brought up his handwriting assignment to be checked. He read aloud this sentence: *If you give a mom a cupcake, she'll ask you for some sprinkles to go with it.*

Potatoes cleaned, baby de-floured, assignments finished, and gravy done, we started dishing out plates and silverware when someone announced a terrible smell coming from the place our geriatric cat had picked as his special spot to leave messes. Vin went to investigate and hollered out, "Can somebody grab Kav? I've got poop on my hand…" and, well, there goes your appetite.

Just another day in Paradise, people. You're welcome.

Not every day is that entertaining, though. Chaos doesn't always come with a sense of humor.

In that season we were navigating heavy situations with ourselves and others, and we noticed that when someone's world is spinning in crisis we tend to ask, "How are you doing?" And there's no answer for that; it's an impossible question. In crisis mode we have no idea how we're doing, and no time or margin to go into the gory details. We face "How are you doing?" like a deer in the headlights.

One of the most important things I've learned is that we need to ask easier, more specific questions. Such as, *Have you had breakfast yet? Can I get you a glass of water? Have you refrained from committing any felonies?*

Another thing I've learned is the grim, settled feeling of leaning in hard to worship when you're tempted to entertain fear or partner with despair. You can't afford to give the enemy a foothold through fear, so instead we push through worship and recognize God's presence.

It's not that we need Him any more than we always do, but we realize we are wholly dependent on Him because seasons like these vividly show us there's no other option. We *must* trust Him.

And when it's my situation, I often wonder how God is going to solve it. Sometimes I get a new idea – *Maybe it'll be this*, I think – and after a brief moment of excitement, I correct myself. *No, no, He won't do it that way, because He won't do it in a way I can predict or expect.* So, great. Now that I've just taken that off the table, His options are really limited...as though He's running out of ideas. Sigh.

It has reminded me many times of the contest between Elijah and the prophets of Baal.[1] You probably know this story; Elijah is a prophet of God and he meets hundreds of false prophets in a showdown at Mount Carmel to prove who the true God was:

> *And Elijah came near to all the people and said, "How long will you go limping between two different opinions? If the Lord is God, follow him; but if Baal, then follow him." And the people did not answer him a word.*
> - 1 Kings 18:21

So, here are the rules they all agreed on: Each side was to sacrifice a bull to their god, but they wouldn't light fire to it. Their god had to provide the fire.

In a move of good sportsmanship, Elijah let the prophets of Baal go first. (Also, my guess is he had a flair for the dramatic, and knew that this would be way cooler when depicted in the movies.)

You know what happens when the prophets called on Baal to light the fire: Nothing. Nothing happens. Elijah, in an early display of snark, starts mocking them and suggests that perhaps Baal is relieving himself somewhere, or asleep.

They go on for hours and nothing happens. They self-mutilate, writhe, scream, and plead, and nothing happens.

(For the record, none of this is what reminds me of our difficult season. I'm getting there.)

Finally Elijah calls the people to him. He repairs the altar of the Lord and makes a trench around it. The wood and the butchered bull go on the altar.

And then he calls for water.

And this is the part that reminds me of our season.

Elijah has the altar, the wood, and the offering all drenched in water. Not just once, but three times, until there was so much water that it filled the trench.

There would be no mistaking which God could bring the fire.

He didn't need perfect circumstances. In fact, the worse the circumstances, the better.

And over those hard months, every time something new hit us, it felt like God was calling for more water to be poured on the altar. I thought, *I know this is still going to work out, but You're letting it look more and more impossible.*

With every bucket of water, we're tempted to ask God what we're doing wrong.

Maybe we should pray differently. But that's what the false prophets did – they worked harder to bring the fire, and the fire still never came.

So what we really need to remember is who (and Who) we're dealing with. It's God's job to bring the fire. It's our job to wait until the water fills the trench.

Elijah didn't pray a fancy prayer.
He just acknowledged God's identity:

> "O Lord, God of Abraham, Isaac, and Israel,"

and then he asked Him to show everyone else who (and Who) they were dealing with:

> *"...let it be known this day that you are God in Israel, and that I am your servant, and that I have done all these things at your word. Answer me, O Lord, answer me, that this people may know that you, O Lord, are God, and that you have turned their hearts back."*
> - 1 Kings 18:36-7

And then God brought the fire.

> *Then the fire of the Lord fell and consumed the burnt offering and the wood and the stones and the dust, and licked up the water that was in the trench.*
> - 1 Kings 18:38

Not only can God bring the fire, but no amount of water on the altar can stop Him from doing it when the time comes. He rewards the obedience of His kids, and He shows people Who they're dealing with.

Elijah didn't want or need any special favors. He already knew he had God's favor. And when you are His kid, obeying Him, leaning into His presence, and worshipping while waiting in the chaos, you have His favor, too.

when the dust settles
BY ROBIN ANGAIAK

All You asked was that I be still. Not inactive, but still.

Trust is still. Trust is both present and productive. Trust is busy becoming the person who can hold the weight of this thing You have promised. Trust is too focused to waste energy trying to hold all the things together.

Time passes and the days grow long. The months turn into years and I begin to wonder if I ever will become. Maybe I am not enough. Maybe You changed Your mind. Maybe I missed the moment.

In all my waiting I have become restless instead of still. My trust has turned inward and the river of hope has been diverted. What once flowed to You is flowing towards a different goal. Where once the end of every promise was more of You, now my soul is demanding an outcome. Some result that satisfies...me.

The River of Diverted Hope is headed to the Valley of Discontent and Never Enough, and I am not still. I am wild and sleepless and everything is out of control. I am grasping and desperate, but not for You. I am desperate for resolution and an end to uncertainty.

I no longer pray to You, but I spend all of my strength on desperation, fear and worry. How much longer must this go on? How much longer can I last?

Broken, angry, ashamed, I turn my heart to You. My tornado blasts into Your throne room, the one I find at the foot of my bed. And You are still. You are in no hurry.

You let the dust settle around me and I see Your face. It is the beginning and end of every promise I have; my inheritance in this life and the next, my peace, my hope.

And then, I hear Your voice.

Beloved, Are you willing to let Me be your hope? Not this promise that you think I am withholding, but Me with you on an adventure? Are you willing to live as though today you will see the breakthrough, even if you don't get to harvest that promise in this life? Are you willing to live content and grateful in this moment, as though every prayer is answered? Because they are – in Me. In My time. In My way. We are just walking it out together.

Lord, I am tired of worrying about how things are going to happen.

You don't have to, I will make it happen.

I'm scared that things will never change and it will always be this way.

But you don't have to stay the same. You can never stay the same when you walk with Me.

I don't think I can do this. I am not good enough; look at what a mess I've made.

I Am enough. I have you. I love you.

What do I do now, Lord?

Be still, trust Me.

To all of us swimming in the deep end of grace – as we let the Lord teach us and lead us in waiting well – may our eyes be ever on Him, as His are on us.

winning the battle

I wrote it on a sticky note and stuck it on the kitchen cabinet that day. And then I wrote it again on our dry erase board, in large enough letters so I could read it across the room:

> *May the God of hope fill you with all joy and peace in believing, so that by the power of the Holy Spirit you may abound in hope.*
> *- Romans 15:13*

It had been 23 hard minutes with a kid who was being equally hard, and this is what we hang on to when it feels like another ten seconds will cook my grits beyond all recognition. *Just engrave this in me, Jesus.*

But a few days later, I could tell someone had been putting in serious prayer for us. I knew it, because we had six kids outside playing in the yard, just like normal, happy kids – and normal, happy, playing togetherness hadn't happened in...I dunno, a year, maybe, or longer. This, friends, was a miracle. It made me almost afraid to blink, to miss it, to hope it was here to stay.

We took it that day with a huge exhale of relief. Reinforcements had arrived, and no one knew how badly we needed them.

We win the battle when we are tempted to resent but we choose to bless and forgive, when we're tempted to despair but choose to hope, or when we're tempted to complain but choose to rejoice. We win by seeing what isn't obviously there – the goodness, the holy work, the future filled with hope. And the only way to see those things is by keeping our eyes on Jesus.

But sometimes the only thing keeping our eyes on Jesus is intercession from others.

It took me a while to realize it, but after a few years of writing I started to recognize that I often experienced spiritual attack in the subject I was writing on. If I was writing about attachment issues, our kids behaviors went through the roof. If it was prayer, I found myself more distracted than ever. And when I wrote the *Work That God Sees* series, I experienced an attack — but also provision — that coincided with the theme of whichever book I was working on.

I felt incapable, and learned I was capable. I experienced a hard time in a friendship, and learned who my allies were. I struggled through growth and grew, I pushed through an emotional season of chaos and He made me steadfast, our family went through difficult circumstances and we learned to be resilient in whole new ways.

When I noticed the pattern, I was actually looking forward to being *Seen*, which was the title of the last book. That sounded easy. And, just being honest, in a marriage of writers, being seen is what helps put food on the table. But on the day I realized I *was* seen, all I really felt was relief that God watches over us, and terror at what could have happened but didn't because God leads others to see and intercede for us, too.

One of our kiddos put himself in an extremely dangerous situation that day, and someone saw him in time. Our family would have never been the same. But God saw, and He prompted someone else to see, and to do something about it.

And all that day He told me to not let the fear and what-might-have-beens take over, because it was a day of sober praise. And He also prompted me to pray for those who had not been seen and had experienced tragedy, not because God didn't see — God always sees us, His eyes are never off us — but because others didn't, and couldn't do something about it.

Those things He prompts you to pray for have eternal impact. It matters every time you pray.

Even when we never see the good that comes of it, even when it feels like we're praying the same thing over and over and we don't know if it does any good...it does. It does good. It does kingdom work.

Pray for your friends. Pray for your neighbors, acquaintances, the strangers you pass on the street. And don't ever stop praying. You never know when the cumulative petition of weeks, months, or years will bear fruit and bring breakthrough that transforms an individual's life and an entire family's future.

This is how we win the battle, and provide hope in the waiting for others.

> *I appeal to you, brothers, by our Lord Jesus Christ and by the love of the Spirit, to strive together with me in your prayers to God on my behalf...*
> *- Romans 15:30*

Pray for your pastors. Pray for the childcare teams and worship leaders. Pray for the ushers and greeters and security crew and coffee shop workers and the media geniuses and the cleaners and everyone else. Some of them are exhausted. Some of them are serving on their only day off. Some of them are running out of gas from serving at high levels and seeing so much pain.

Praying for them brings necessary reinforcements to those who are hungry and tired from hard marching, and it helps us all advance the kingdom.

Sometimes our prayer brings the huge victory, but most of the time it's just the difference between tragedy and ho-hum ordinary days. If we had any idea how often God used our prayers for our own protection and the protection of others, we'd never stop.

unexpected terrain

It was our first visit to Hatcher Pass in two years. It is my favorite place in the world; we were with close friends; we planned to park and take a quick hike and then drive back home for dinner.

That's the way it was supposed to go, at least.

On the way to the parking lot we were stopped by a new fee station, and quickly discovered that since our last visit, some group of political geniuses decided to start taxing the upper parking area with a new per-person fee. And our party consisted of two vehicles and seventeen people.

So we collectively decided to take the cheaper $5 option and we parked where we were. Just a little more exercise, we thought; no biggie. We had planned for a short ninety minute hike, and this would just add a little time to it.

Ha. Two hours later we were still wandering up the tundra and we hadn't even made it to the trailhead, which we could see in the not-too-far-off distance. Some of the bigger kids went way up the mountain in the wrong direction, and we yelled and flagged them down before they went over the pass toward Canada.

It was already dinner time, and home was still thirty minutes away…from the parking lot…which was all the way back down.

It wasn't supposed to be this way. It was supposed to be a scenic walk of less than a mile, with a little incline toward the end; it was supposed to terminate at a glorious lake hidden in a shelf of the mountain until you practically stumble into it, with an incredible view of the whole valley behind us.

> *The point is, can God really put a doubt in us who have believed? If the Lord tells you that this delay is for His glory, then you must take victory in it. There is no glory in delay, unless there was faith to put it through....Very strange that what is death in the eyes of the world, is victory to the Holy Spirit.*
> *- Norman Grubb* [2]

So many things are not the way we planned, expected, or prayed for. Life gets rerouted: Marriages hit a quagmire and threaten to go under. Kids make hard choices and the consequences affect everyone. Relationships, health, or milestones go awry. This is not how it was supposed to be.

I finished reading a biography on Rees Howells around that time, and they, too, saw things go as they didn't seem they were supposed to:

> *It was the first lesson for many...whether they can walk through their valley of humiliation, of apparent failure, with an unmoved faith. The very thing they believed for did not come to pass....It seemed the end of Gospel work in the country. But Mr. Howells explained to [them] the principle that has already been referred to: that apparent failure may only be a stepping-stone to greater victory.*
> *- Norman Grubb* [3]

We gave up on the lake and decided to go back. I was already badly sunburned and on the way down the mountain my left knee started throbbing. It screamed, *I'm in my forties, have mercy!* while the rest of my body yelled, *Suck it up, you can do this! The parking lot is another thousand feet away and if you give out now, we'll all pay the consequences!*

We hiked over streams hidden in shrubbery. The ground was broken open, exposed as a conduit to receive water so it can send life and healing further down the mountain.

And this is the way it is with us: Sometimes we need to break before we can be healed deeply.

Without pushing through that hard healing, unexposed grime festers and affects generations to come. I won't lie, I know how terrible it is. It's like having your vitals scrubbed, and sometimes we don't know if we'll survive it.

We break when we give up our expectations of the way we thought things would be for the way things actually are.

We break through hard confession and repentance (whether we are the one confessing, or we're the one hearing it for the first time). It's an exposure none of us ever want to go through, but the infection underneath has to be cleaned out before it's too late.

And we break when we realize that what God asks of us is sometimes very different than what we thought we signed up for.

But it's necessary to reset what was already broken and hidden underneath. Whether it was intentional or not, or whether it was a result of our own choices or someone else's, we need to see where we've gone off course so we can make an accurate correction and move forward. And sometimes the way forward is actually going back. And it is so hard. We think it's failure – and sometimes it is, but not always. Even if it is failure, it doesn't always mean that's the end of the trail.

> *...if our prayers were of faith, we have only had a setback, and not a failure as a result of unbelief.*
> *- Norman Grubb* [4]

We don't know what's going to happen in the painful events around us. Personally, several years into our marriage we didn't know it would survive the breaking and scouring we went through. We had to work through the waiting as we walked toward healing. And more recently, we don't know if we'll ever see the full healing we've hoped for in two of our children.

But we do know that when we trust Him and push through the hard stuff, we are moving forward...even if we're not on the path we thought we'd be on.

It took years before Rees Howells saw the victory after their apparent failure:

> *God's answer was perfect. The expansion of missionary work in the country...has been by far the greatest in its history. Just as it was to be later in the World War, so now, the answer to intercession could not have been complete until the aggressor had been so dealt with that he could not rise up and menace the country again; and when the missionaries returned...they could not account for the revival which had been going on...when some 500 converts had increased to 20,000.*
> *- Norman Grubb* [5]

Healing through this kind of failure is what qualifies us for the bigger victory. Living through recovery is what gives our ministry a greater impact, our leadership a greater influence, and our credentials more validity.

If I was looking for marriage counseling, I wouldn't get it from people who have always had a perfect marriage. And if I wanted parenting advice, I wouldn't ask someone who's never experienced extreme challenges with their kids.

If I need help in any area – ministry, family, business, relationships, whatever – I want it from people who know what it's like to go to hell and back, and are now thriving in humility and a deeper understanding of what the terrain is like. I want someone who's gained their expertise through trusting God in the middle of what looks and feels like failure, and made it through the scrubbing.

I want people who were willing to push through the pain rather than let the rest of the body carry the consequences. These are the people creating a legacy of grit and honor for generations to come. And if you are in a hard place right now, hoping in the waiting and pushing through the pain, you are one of them.

rooted in hope

BY CYNTHIA HELLMAN

I live in a desert. Trees are a rare sight. Well, let me preface that: We have trees, but they're scrubby things. I'm talking about *trees* trees. I mean the tall, feel-like-a-speck-when-you-stand-and-look-up-at-them variety. Majestic evergreens — redwood, fir, pine...

We have one palo verde tree flourishing along our wash. We have a second palo verde tree dying along our wash (thank you, palo verde beetles). Oh, that's right...not everyone lives in the desert. Um, imagine small rivers. Now replace the water with dirt. That's a wash. When we get a gullywasher of a storm, the wash becomes a river for a day or so. And we all look on in wonder...but I digress. One palo verde provides welcome shade from the harsh summer sun. The other is an eyesore, probably dragging down the neighborhood housing market prices. Neither are particularly magnificent to behold compared to a mighty oak tree.

Desert plants are a funny thing; they're the camel of horticulture. The saguaro takes advantage of summer monsoons to soak up as much moisture as possible. Their skins swell to contain the extra nourishment, storing it for dry seasons. Conversely, transplanted palo verdes are typically damaged in our summer monsoons. Housing developments and businesses oftentimes plant palo verde trees for aesthetics and parking shade. Then they proceed to overwater the poor things. Monsoons hit, and the waterlogged palo verdes snap, uproot, and are swept away.

Just like the saguaro, palo verdes need the dry seasons. In the parched times both develop mature root systems. Without those triple digit temperatures, the desert flora won't push through our stubborn soil to find water. If there's no need to dig deeper, they simply celebrate their shallow roots...until the first good monsoon storm splinters their illusion of strength.

The wild palo verdes withstand the gales much better than those planted along medians and parking spots. They've grown stronger in times of scarcity; no drip-system provided what they sought. Thirsty tendrils stretched out in search of water, reaching farther than their transplanted, spoon-fed counterparts.

A drip-system faith may look promising; it offers much, but leaves us weak and indefensible against a vile destroyer. The temporal pulls our eyes off the sustainer and author of life. We look to modern comforts for the solution to age-old sin. We try on shortcuts to satisfy our hope instead of trusting the One who knit those desires in us from the beginning of time.

Sometimes we don't even know what we need. We might

know what we want — what we long to see actualized. Sometimes we aren't even sure if what we're hoping for is what God has for us, amen? What then? When we aren't sure what we need or what we dare hope for, that's when what we *truly* need is to push through the discomfort and filth to sit at His feet.

Anchored. Nourished.

The only source that can sustain us in times of drought, when hope is thin, is the Living Water. And the only way to find Him is to plow through the worn out tropes and dry facade.
It's a narrow way which leads to the Living Water. But He supplies all our needs and intimately knows our secret (and not-so-secret) hopes. After all, hope is faith wrapped in God-sized dreams.

Hopeless waiting is passive and stagnant. It looks like sitting, staring at drip-systems, twiddling spiritual thumbs while waiting for the next exciting revelation. God's people are called to something bolder and more vibrant — something active and counter-cultural. Hope-filled waiting may look passive, but heavy lifting is going on under the surface. Waiting is swollen with the Holy Spirit's touch. The real work is done when there's hope in the waiting. For when the deluge rolls over us, it can no more uproot us than a grain of sand could command the waves.

how we hold our ground

I felt aimless, trying to write, trying to finish a piece I was working on. And instead of doing anything remotely productive (*like removing the adverb "remotely," the writer scolded herself*) I was scrolling, refreshing internet pages, clipping my nails, flipping through books, trying to find something, anything, that would spark a new thought and somehow bring everything together. But no luck so far.

The words were congealing and clogging up; I had some content but no illustrations to pull everything into a cohesive story. So I set the timer for ten minutes and pushed myself back into the journal, turning the writerly faucet on full blast to run the muck out and see if the water would start running clear by the time the alarm went off.

It's what I'd have my writing students do. Sometimes we have to teach ourselves, too.

I spent much of the ten minutes resisting the urge to see how much time was left. I'd take a drink of water, sigh loudly, and notice my hand cramping. Vin had taken the kids out of the house to do some grocery shopping, so it was just me and the cats at home – the perfect stereotype of the slightly obsessive, extremely reclusive, eccentric writer.

The timer went off, and the pen skidded off the page as I jumped.

But it worked. The water was running clear again, and I got up to refill my glass before tackling another page.

Another thing that often works is switching gears to work on something else. When we're stalled on one thing, we can at least take a different tack and make some progress on something else. And usually, it's a good option – progress is progress, right?

But sometimes progress isn't the point, because movement is only good if it's in the right direction.

So in some cases (*like when you have a deadline*, the writer thought, looking at the clock) continuing to put off one task in favor of something shinier is not going to help you get it done. Sometimes we just have to stick with it and push through.

And we are in a season of pushing through. Maybe you are, too. Not too long ago, our family had some choices to make, and we realized those choices came down to two things: We could take the traditional, secure route, which seemed easier in some ways, but it also felt like striving and capitulating to fear. Or we could push through in faith, and wait, trusting that God's answer was not in the wider, smoother, well-traveled path, but in the bracken where He'd placed us.

*For the Lord knows the way of the righteous,
but the way of the wicked will perish.*
- Psalm 1:6

When we realized those were our options, the answer seemed clearer. Not any easier, of course, just more peaceful. And peace brings its own kind of ease that a smooth path doesn't.

He has answers for us in the bracken if we're willing to stand our ground in it and trust Him.

He wasn't saying, *No, don't leave for the wide path*; He was offering us something better if we would stay and hold on. He would be with us in either place, but if we were brave enough to wait, He'd lead us to a view we never could have found by leaving this path in the bracken, where we couldn't see what was ahead. He could see what was ahead, and we chose to trust that it was as good as He said it was.

Isn't that what obedience and surrender always come down to, though? Sometimes we think God is telling us no, but it's never about the No. He is always offering a bigger Yes.

For this light momentary affliction is preparing for us an eternal weight of glory beyond all comparison, as we look not to the things that are seen but to the things that are unseen. For the things that are seen are transient, but the things that are unseen are eternal.
- 2 Corinthians 4:17-18

We heard, *Hold on, and you'll be glad you did.* The only way we can hold on is with hope – that concrete, weighty grip that should never be mistaken for something fluffy, because hope means we understand He is who He says He is, and He does what He says He'll do.

Hope is a form of worship because it acknowledges God and declares He is trustworthy. And our worship is warfare, because hope is the element of surprise that scrambles the communications of the enemy and confuses his ranks.

That enemy whispers, "Give up. Lower your weapons."
And we respond, "Fire."
- Oh My Soul [6]

These hope-filled people are dangerous, reckless, unpredictable, capable of anything. They are the ones who follow their Leader.

He's still asking me, *Do you want the plan, or do you want the power?* [7] And that's a no brainer, even for a planner like me.

We don't want to run from what He wants to teach us. So we push through this murky part of the path, following closely on His heels so we don't get lost. Yes, we keep looking at the clock. Yes, sometimes we cramp in the close quarters. And yeah, sometimes we sigh and wish the timer would just go off.

But He's said that clarity is just around the corner, and we believe Him.

shining through

I took half a dozen pictures of the sunset, and the few minutes between photos made them look like half a dozen different sunsets – gold, orange, fuchsia, purple, all the blues in the world.

And here's the thing I learned about sunsets that night: The stuff that makes the colors visible is there all along. The molecules and particles that make those colors are there when the sun is high, but we just don't see them. The sun has to get lower and lower – and then drop out entirely – before we see those amazing colors.

And if you feel like your light has gone out, you don't have any answers, you're out of ideas, and everything is threatening to go very dark, consider this: Everything we need is still right here. God has unexpected color and answers and joy for you in this time, and He is positioning things so you can start to see them.

You, oh children of Light, are made brighter and more beautiful for all the dirt and clouds you've had to shine through.

Do not fear the darkness. The world is not going to drop out from under you. He has you firmly held. The sun is going to rise again soon. And He has more color to show you then, too.

In a season when I desperately needed color, the Lord led me to Luke 1:45, a verse I didn't have memorized. And by "the Lord led me to it" I don't mean I happened to stumble upon the verse while I was reading the book of Luke. I mean, it was a series of only-God-could-have-done-that coincidences that He made very obvious so I couldn't possibly ignore them, and it spoke exactly to something I had been praying about. Here it is:

> *And blessed is she who believed that there would be a fulfillment of what was spoken to her from the Lord.*
> - Luke 1:45

You can bet I've memorized the verse by now. And even now, He keeps bringing it up, asking me if I'll keep believing for big things, trusting Him more than ever, regardless of what things look like.

Will I look to the gorgeous view? Or will I focus on the dirty window between me and that view — or on the warped reflection of what's behind me?

Now is a time to be asking God for a bigger vision, for the next dream, for a clearer picture of the calling He's placed on your life. This is a time for looking forward, not shrinking back.

> *Therefore the Lord waits to be gracious to you,*
> *and therefore he exalts himself to show mercy to you.*
> *For the Lord is a God of justice;*
> *blessed are all those who wait for him.*
> - Isaiah 30:18

He waits, and we wait, and He blesses us for it. And I'm noticing here that He doesn't ask us to do anything He hasn't done Himself.

What if our bad news, our bombshells, our curveballs, were really good news in the long run? What if they were really for our favor, on our behalf, and resulted in a smack in the face of the enemy?

> *The Lord is near to the brokenhearted*
> *and saves the crushed in spirit.*
> *Many are the afflictions of the righteous,*
> *but the Lord delivers him out of them all.*
> *- Psalm 34:7, 17-19*

He doesn't have you stuck in the slow lane; you're not stuck at all. He has you in a place of rest so He can move through you. Things are going on behind the scenes and under the surface that are in your favor, for your great joy. Just because you can't see them yet doesn't change the reality of their existence.

Whatever breakthrough you've been praying for, He hears you, He sees you, and He is working things out for your good, even (especially) when it's hard.

> *And we know that for those who love God all*
> *things work together for good, for those who are*
> *called according to his purpose.*
> *- Romans 8:28*

God is a healer, deliverer, and beauty bringer, and we could not contain our excitement if we fully knew what He is up to in our situations. He is moving on our behalf, bringing justice, revival, and breakthrough as we surrender to Him.

So get in the Word, and get your hopes up.

The enemy feeds on fear and lies and despair. They're practically his only weapons and they only work if people believe them. Hope brighter, stay in the Word, pray without ceasing. Those are unbeatable weapons, and the enemy is terrified of them.

These are days for learning more, loving deeply, praying hard, trusting God, leaning into scripture, practicing grace and repentance, forgiving and pressing on, discerning the times and asking for wisdom, speaking truth in love, and pushing through in obedience to the task in front of us.

These are not days to walk recklessly, impulsively, succumbing to our own knee jerk reactions, or to the pressure or enthusiasm of those without a plumb line for truth.

These are days to remember God is so very near to us, willing to speak and counsel, to correct and comfort, to bring hope and heal.

Just like every day. But we bear better fruit in these days when we remember it.

hope is the thing with feathers

BY EMILY DICKINSON, 1830-1886

Hope is the thing with feathers
That perches in the soul,
And sings the tune without the words,
And never stops at all,

And sweetest in the gale is heard;
And sore must be the storm
That could abash the little bird
That kept so many warm.

I've heard it in the chillest land,
And on the strangest sea;
Yet, never, in extremity,
It asked a crumb of me.

waiting for home
BY JESSICA DASSOW

A thoughtful friend sent me an article this morning. It was kind of her to think of me, and the article itself was true in every way and resonated deeply with me. The author described her uneasiness and unsettledness in the face of various moves – her realization there would never be a true settledness here, because as a Christian, this world is not her home. So if the post was true (it was), and it spoke to my heart because I relate so much to the author's personal experience (it did), then why was it discouraging to me to read her words? Why, instead of feeling encouragement, did my eyes sting with tears and my heart feel rubbed raw?

With these thoughts in my mind, I decided to go run it out with Jesus, because that's how I tend to handle moments like these. I knew the condemnation and guilt were not from Him because that's just not how He operates, and I needed to get *His* perspective on the matter.

I stepped out into the brilliant, frosty morning, my emotions sending my feet flying before I even reached the driveway.

"Why does this bother me so much?!" I may or may not have exclaimed this to all of Spring Valley, but really my question was only directed toward one Person. "I mean, I absolutely know You are 'home' and the only 'home' I was truly meant for. And the truth is, I would choose YOU over 1000 'perfect homes' here on Earth. But LORD, this still hurts! Is that okay?!" My Asics came to a halt on the country road's pavement.

And then I realized it. It stung because I had had a similar post reeling around in my mind for a long, long while. My yet-to-be-written post, though different because it shared my own story, imparted the same message – we will never feel truly at home this side of Heaven because this world is not our home.

> *These all died in faith, not having received the things promised, but having seen them and greeted them from afar, and having acknowledged that they were strangers and exiles on the earth. For people who speak thus make it clear that they are seeking a homeland. If they had been thinking of that land from which they had gone out, they would have had opportunity to return. But as it is, they desire a better country, that is, a heavenly one. Therefore God is not ashamed to be called their God, for he has prepared for them a city.*
> *- Hebrews 11:13-16*

And that's the truth. I know it. I believe it. I experience it. But the post in my mind remained unwritten, even in my personal journals. Why? Because I didn't feel ready (qualified?) to share. You see, though I know and believe that truth with every ounce of my soul, I'm still hurting. I'm still struggling, and I'm still watching my husband and children struggle. I guess I thought in order to write that post I should be clean-pressed and confident, smiling over the joy and peace that rules my life. And while I'm confident of this truth deep in my soul, there's still the daily life logistics to contend with. To wrestle with. And perhaps I thought I needed to be completely at ease with the mess in order to be qualified to share my reeling-in-my-mind blog post. I wanted to cleanly and confidently wrap that post up with a perfectly-tied bow instead of feeling like an imposter. But as I stood silently on Spring Valley Road staring up into the sky, the reality hit that I couldn't. That I'm a mess.

We've been settled Earth-side before. We know what that's like, and we long to experience it again. No, it wasn't perfect. And we didn't expect it to be. But it was home. It was a sense of comfort which made the day-to-day details of working and living and raising a family easier. However, even with that sense of comfort we had when we were home, there was still a nagging sense of unsettledness, knowing of "this isn't final" and that "we were made for something more." And it was ok. I'm forever thankful for that nagging sense, because it pointed me to Christ then and it points me to Him now. I need that reminder of my true Home, my true Comfort, my Sufficiency.

So yes – the post I read this morning? I totally get it. I live it every day in my present season of still struggling to find home after nearly five years, and it means more to me than ever before. But still, I never wrote the message myself. And now I realize it's because I'm wrestling with the fact that I'm hurting and discouraged even though I know and believe the truth. Does that mean I don't actually know and believe the truth?

The sun cascaded down on my frosty breath and I ran waaay faster than usual. (Wrestling with the LORD is good for the physical form, yes?) I felt Him speak to my heart, "It's okay that you're hurting and struggling even in the midst of believing and trusting me. I don't expect you to shut off your feelings. Knowing and trusting doesn't mean you don't feel. I don't expect you to pretend it's all okay."

> *Now faith is the assurance of things hoped for, the conviction of things not seen.*
> *- Hebrews 11:1*

At that moment I realized I had expected myself to be a rockstar Believer. I had wanted to be able to share my struggles but then point to our Sufficiency and smile, saying, "Look! I'm totally okay and I feel so awesome because the truth is this world is not our home!" Except that wouldn't be honest. Because I don't feel okay. Maybe someday I will, but I'm not there yet. So instead, I'm going to be honest and share that we will always feel like strangers in a strange land because this world is not our home, yes…but sometimes life circumstances make the struggle

seem even more so. Does this resonate with you?

For me at present, it looks like living out of boxes, kids growing up like wildfire amidst chaos, and anticipating the need to pack up yet a fifth time whenever we find that healthy landing place this side of Heaven. The daily tasks of living are extra arduous because half of the kitchen is in storage, and no, it doesn't feel very homey when we wake to something gnawing (WHAT) up in the wall of our 1905 farmhouse rental, and, oh yes! We can't make a permanent solution for the uranium in the water coming out of our sink.

There are hard emotions that accompany these things. Yes, we are so thankful for this provision of a roof and walls and water and a gorgeous view and loved neighbors. But no, it's not all puppies and rainbows, and THANK THE HOLY LORD we don't have to pretend it is. And so we hurt. And we struggle. It doesn't make our faith in the Person who is our home any less. It doesn't steal away the deep soul peace we have in knowing Who is in charge and that He is good. We can be honest about the hard while still being thankful for present provision and trusting the Giver's good for us and our future.

How about you? I'm guessing it's not all puppies and rainbows for you, either? Whatever life is throwing at you right now, there is deep, soul peace to be had. And you can have that soul peace and things may still not look real pretty or feel very good on the outside. And that's okay. We don't have to pretend. Page through the Psalms and you'll see we're not alone in the struggling. And if you, too, are feeling like a bit of a mess even though you know and believe He's got your back, it's okay. And furthermore, you're in good company, because so many of us are weathering the storm and feeling the same way.

I'm so glad my friend sent me that link this morning. It was the push I needed to confront my current struggles more honestly. I hope it encourages you to do the same.

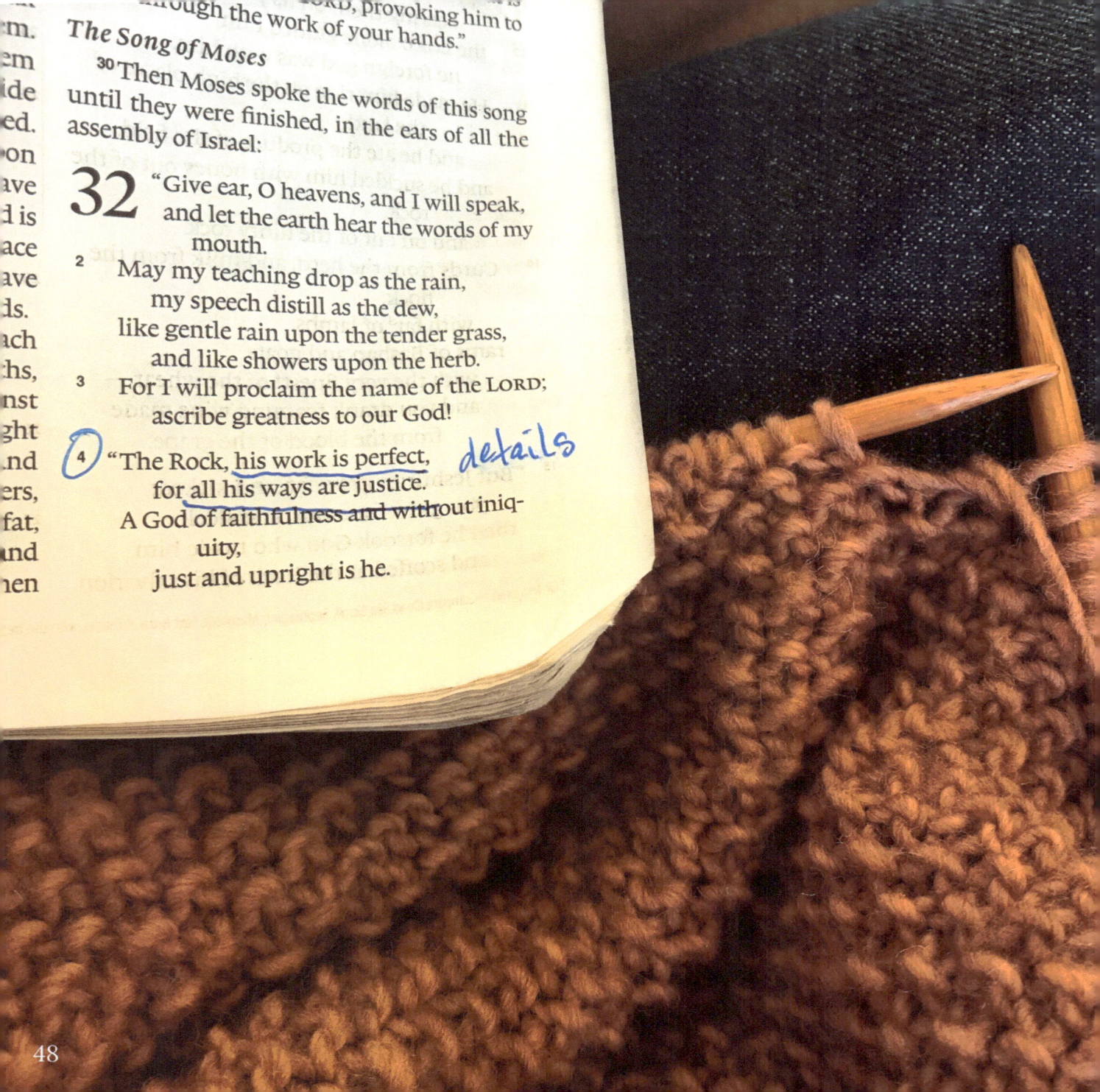

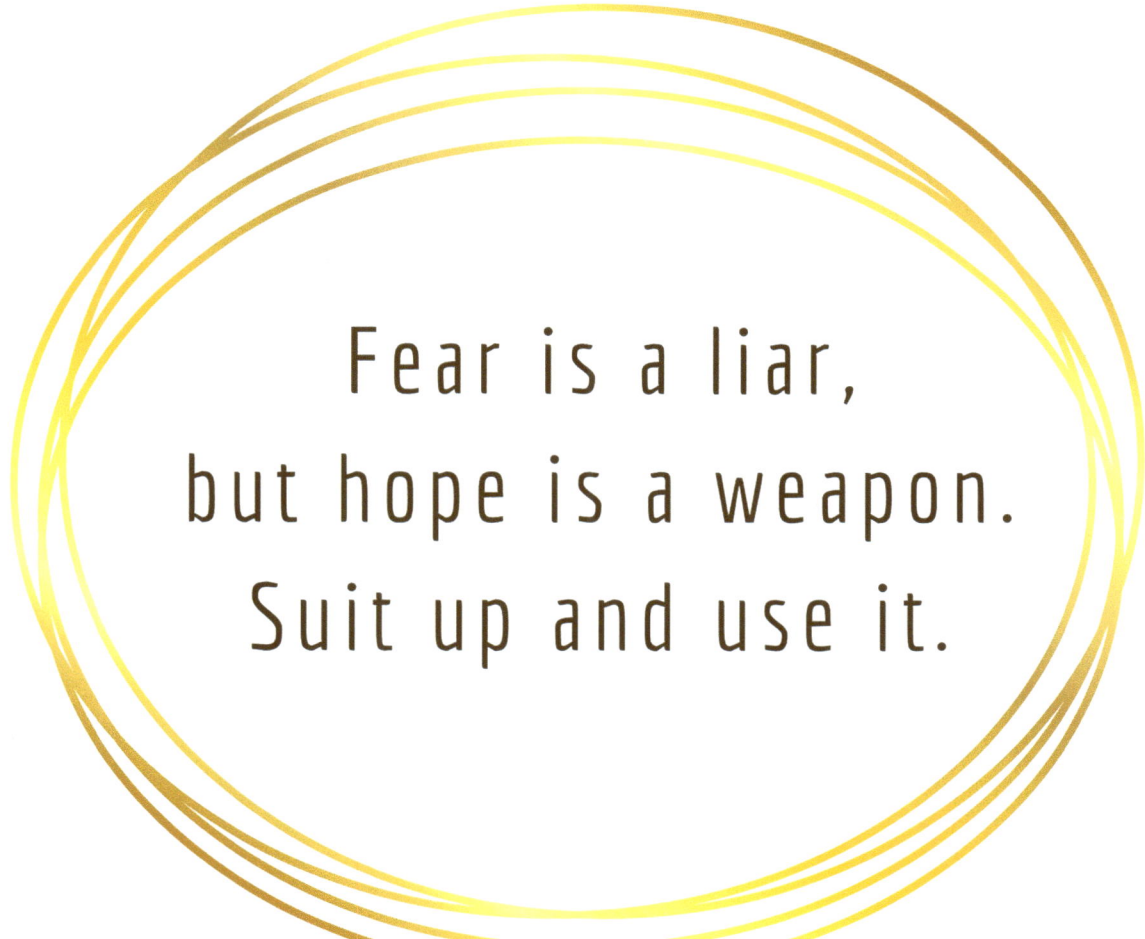

Fear is a liar,
but hope is a weapon.
Suit up and use it.

budding

In early spring, the trees are pregnant with buds and pussy willows. They were made to grow, to have seasons of rest and rebirth. And so are we.

But if we were living through our first spring and we had no idea that summer was ahead, would we be satisfied with these tiny leaves for long? How would we know there were full, lush leaves to look forward to?

Would we get angsty and restless over the brown grass and wispy branches, longing for full shade and greenery everywhere?

Or would we rest in the small growth, knowing that a good God who makes cold, naked branches bud green leaves can also make those same leaves break out in fullness that we could never imagine for ourselves?

Budding things are all around me: kids, young adults, books, ministries, businesses, ideas. Many of them seem small, wayward, insignificant, or just not growing...to me, at least. But in many ways, this is still my first spring. I've never seen how big some of these budding leaves can get.

When our toddler was just tall enough to reach the doorknob, he knew that touching it had something to do with opening the door. He just couldn't figure out how to make it work. Ever feel that way?

Obedience and hard work aren't enough to open the door. It sure feels like it ought to be, though.

Often, we also just need time. And time means waiting, and waiting is not sexy. It feels helpless. It pushes my buttons. It makes me run around, striving, trying harder, until I realize what's happening. I waste time in the striving and fussing when I could be enjoying life, playing with the toys I can reach, trusting God with the process of growth.

When the trees are bare in winter, do they know that they will be bigger and broader, reaching higher and further, in just a few months?

When there was void and darkness, when there was no outline, He hovered. He brooded.[8] He waited for the right time and then these five words happened:

~ in the beginning God created ~

And He's still doing it. Do you see those buds? They're like filigree. Guys, we're so close.

When there is darkness, when we are at a loss and without answers – when we are brooding and waiting and restless, desperate for breakthrough, He is hovering. He is saying, *Just you wait, Love. I haven't even started yet.*

Friend, I want you to think of that old back-burner prayer you've shoved aside and given up on. The one that seems to be doing nothing, the one you've left for dead. This is the time to grab that thing and dust it off.

Take it back to God. Tell Him you haven't forgotten. Confess that you know He hasn't forgotten you, either.

And pray that prayer again – for the dream, for the breakthrough, for the lost one you've stopped hoping for. Tell that mountain to move like you're the boss of it. You *are* the boss of it; you're the steward of the King.

Pray like a tree who knows that it doesn't matter how bare the branches are in the winter — spring is coming, and God has made you to reach further than you ever have before. It is your

beginning. And in the beginning, God creates. It will be greater than you imagine.

And then, when we've done everything else we need to do, we won't force the issue. We will move on to something else and let God finish working it out. When we can't get anything done, He is still and always doing. There's a mess of new, baby leaves out there trumpeting new life and goodness.

He will let us know when it's time to try to turn the doorknob again. He loves it when we reach for Him first.

whispered hope
BY RENEE PETTY

Let Hope reign in my life

    On the longest of nights,

For you are there in the dark

    Speaking truth to my heart.

Trust in me, my beloved, the morning will come.

hash browns
with jalapeño aioli

I love All Things Potato but I am ~~particularly fond of~~ slightly obsessed with these hash browns. In our house, they pass for breakfast, lunch, dinner, and date night.

Ingredients:
One large potato, shredded
¼-½ onion, shredded (depends on how much you like onions)
Salt
Pepper
Olive oil
Butter

1. Put the shredded potato and onion into a mesh sieve and drain the liquid into the sink. It helps to use the bottom of a glass and press the mixture to squeeze out as much moisture as possible.

2. Using a large cast iron or stainless steel skillet (whichever you're most comfortable with), coat the bottom of the skillet with about ½ tablespoon of olive oil – not a thick layer, but use a metal spatula to gently spread the oil around, making sure to edge it up the sides a little ways. You'll thank me later when you get to flipping.

3. Turn the heat to medium and wait for the oil to get hot. Test it by flicking a drop of water into it; if it sizzles, you're in business. DO NOT PROCEED UNTIL IT SIZZLES. Trust me on this.

4. Pour the potato & onion mixture into the pan – hear that amazing sizzling sound? That's good news. Quickly spread the mixture over the bottom of the pan without disturbing the stuff that is touching the bottom of the pan and sizzling. It is creating that beautiful golden sear that makes hash browns superior to almost every other potato dish.

5. Press the mixture flat with your spatula. You should hear more loud sizzling. You're doing great.

6   Wait a few minutes until you see the edges of the potato start to brown a little. Add a little butter around the edges, or to anywhere it looks like the hash browns need some extra oil. This is a good time to sprinkle salt and pepper on the uncooked side; this is a very *bad* time to preemptively wedge your spatula under the potatoes and attempt flipping. Don't even try it. Resist, I tell you.

7   Once you see some golden color appearing on the edges, you can start to flip. Depending on your skill and the size of your spatula, you can do it all at once or in sections (I do it in sections, no shame). Using the sharp edge of your spatula or a dull butter knife, divide the hash browns by pressing right into the mixture (fourths are good). Got it? Ready? Okay, flip!

8   YAYYY. You should be looking at a beautiful mess of golden shredded potato. Add a little more butter or oil to the pan and let the undersides cook for a few minutes while you prep your aioli and do a victory dance.

jalapeño aioli

ingredients:
¼ cup mayonnaise
1/8 t. cayenne
1 T chopped jalapeños (I like to use the fermented ones)
1T lemon juice or apple cider vinegar (or the brine from the fermented jalapeños, if you're using them)
For bonus points, add a pinch of dill or chopped fresh chives.

Mix together. Use as a dip for All Things Potato – hash browns, fries, chips, baked potatoes. And if you tend to replace sweet potatoes for potatoes, it works well with them, too.

bakery style double chocolate muffins

BY MĒGAN ANCHETA makes 12-14 muffins

I'm a sucker for chocolate muffins, especially the ones you see in bakeries with all the melty chocolate chips. If you're anything like me, this recipe will easily satisfy that craving!

ingredients:
1/2 cup sorghum flour
1/2 cup brown rice flour
1/2 cup tapioca starch
1/3 cup cocoa powder
1 teaspoon baking soda
1/2 teaspoon xanthan gum
1/2 teaspoon sea salt
3/4 cup unsweetened applesauce
3/4 cup olive oil (or melted coconut oil)
1/2 cup honey
2 large eggs
1/2 cup dairy-free chocolate mini chips

1. Preheat oven to 350 degrees (F).

2. In the bowl of an electric mixer, combine the sorghum flour, brown rice flour, tapioca starch, cocoa powder, baking soda, xanthan gum and sea salt.

3. In a separate mixing bowl, combine the unsweetened applesauce, olive oil, honey, and eggs.

4. Pour the dry ingredients into the wet, and mix until the batter is smooth.

5. Mix in the dairy-free chocolate mini chips.

6 Divide the batter into 12-14 paper lined muffin tins, filling each 3/4 full. Bake for 16-20 minutes, or until a toothpick comes out clean when inserted into the middle of a muffin (be careful not to overbake).

7 Cool completely before enjoying.

Recipe Notes:
You can add up to a cup of chopped nuts to the batter if desired.

When I have it on hand, I also like to add espresso powder to this batter. There's nothing better than coffee and chocolate!

what leads to victory

It was dark out and the roads were icy, and Vince still wasn't home from his commute. An hour and a half earlier he had texted that he was on his way, and it was only an hour drive. So being cool and level-headed, I spent the extra thirty minutes trying not to imagine which ditch he was in and whether or not his car could be seen from an embankment if he had flipped upside down.

Then he finally texted me: He had stopped at the store, but would be home in ten minutes. What a relief. And because I am romantic and sentimental, I texted him back:

> Don't ever die on me, I hate grocery shopping.

The snarky sense of humor might be a spiritual gift. God certainly has it; one of the things He speaks to me about the most is how to deal with fear, discouragement, and anxiety ...and then He often tells me to *share* those things on video or in public, so I can practice what I preach when it comes to fear, anxiety, and discouragement. Super fun. (Cringe.)

But here's what I'm learning: We are called to be still, not to strive; to wait and listen, not to

rush and worry; to focus less on our own imperfections and more on His perfection; to trust His hold on our situations and seasons, instead of grasping and flailing for control.

What comes out of us reflects what we allow to go into us, and stress can reveal this like nothing else. So if you are fighting fear or anxiety, check what you are filling yourself up with. If you are discouraged or despairing, look to the right things (hint: the news is not one of them). How can we nurture peace in our hearts so that is what comes out of us when fear, anxiety, or discouragement come calling?

More books. More scripture. Less social media. Less mainstream media. More conversations. More prayer. Less imagining the worst-case scenario. More imagining what breakthrough will look like. Less fretting, less anger. More worship, more prayer. More rest.

These lead to more trusting God, which leads to more victory.

> *For this reason I bow my knees before the Father, from whom every family in heaven and on earth is named, that according to the riches of his glory he may grant you to be strengthened with power through his Spirit in your inner being...*
> - Ephesians 3:14-16

If our life is a conduit (and it is) then fear and fretting clog it up. Disobedience clogs it up. Unforgiveness clogs it up.

But abiding is the antidote.

> ...so that Christ may dwell in your hearts through faith—that you, being rooted and grounded in love, may have strength to comprehend with all the saints what is the breadth and length and height and depth, and to know the love of Christ that surpasses knowledge, that you may be filled with all the fullness of God.
> - Ephesians 3:17-19

We abide and obey, and focus on what He is doing (because He is always doing) and that gives Him room to move in our situation in spite of all our previous angstiness.

He loves having room to move. Abiding and surrender give it to Him.

Some things will be worse than you expect, true. But that's no reason to dread them or lose hope, because some things will also be so much better than we could have imagined. Dread and pessimism are flimsy weapons; hope-grounded faith is undefeated.

> *Now to him who is able to do far more abundantly than all that we ask or think, according to the power at work within us, to him be glory in the church and in Christ Jesus throughout all generations, forever and ever. Amen.*
> - Ephesians 3:20-21

Not everything is as urgent as it seems to be, because my deadlines aren't always based on God's timeline. We have more time than we think. If something is taking longer than we thought it would, it doesn't mean failure. It means growth. And that is its own achievement.

As we ask Him, God will prune the dead stuff off us, and it can be hard and messy. But there will also be a strong sense of the turning of a corner, like He's about to show us what He's been up to.

Hey Love, He asks us, *Are you ready to start praying in color again for things you've only been praying for in tones of grey?*

He is not waiting for us to figure it all out. If we need a miracle, it is not going to come from us suddenly figuring it all out. That wouldn't be a miracle at all – and we would be tempted to take credit for it, anyway. When we're walking in radical obedience, the miracle comes out of the blue, out of left field, out of what we thought was nowhere, no-how, never saw that coming. It is an Ephesians 3:20 powerhouse, breaking through despair and discouragement and worries. It will surpass all our ideas and expectations and patterns of what we think is supposed to happen.

And we should get ready for it.

faithfulness springs up
from the ground,
and *righteousness* looks down from the sky.
Yes, the Lord will give what is good,
and our land will yield its increase.
Righteousness will go before him
and make his footsteps a way.

- psalm 85:11-13

study guide

This flexible, light-yoked guide is for you to use on your own or with a small group. We've included questions to use for personal journaling or group discussion, scripture to study, copy down, and memorize, and short prompts for prayer. It's not homework or another thing to add to your list – it's just movement forward and rest for your soul, friends.

come hungry

questions

Where in my life does it feel like I'm having hot water for dinner?

What might God be preparing that I can't see?

What would a feast look like in that situation?

scripture

Psalm 84:6-7, Luke 1:46-55

prayer

Lord, I know You are doing more than I can see or imagine. Help me to pray in cooperation with You and worship while I wait.

we know Who brings the fire

questions

What have I been praying for that feels like it just keeps getting more and more impossible?

How can I move out of God's way and express my trust for Him in this?

How am I leaning into His presence and worshipping in this season?

scripture

1 Kings 18

prayer

God, you are the one in charge, and there is nothing that can stop you from moving. Show us Your mighty power and faithfulness in this situation.

when the dust settles

questions

What fears and concerns do I need to be honest with God about?

What does He say in response?

What do stillness and trust look like in my life?

scripture

Ecclesiastes 4:6, Hebrews 4:14-16

prayer

Lord, You are not afraid of my honesty and You already know what is in my heart. Help me to come to You without shame or fear, so I can lay everything before you and hear Your words for me.

winning the battle

questions

Where am I tempted to resent, and can bless and forgive instead?

Where am I tempted to despair and complain, but can rejoice and hope instead?

Who can I intercede for right now?

scripture

Romans 15:8-33

prayer

Holy Spirit, help me see those who need prayer. Help me to walk in forgiveness and joy as I look toward the future.

unexpected terrain

questions

In what area of my life do I need to go back for healing so I can move forward in hope?

What might need to be broken first so that healing can happen there?

What is the next step I need to take to cooperate with that healing?

scripture

1 Corinthians 1:3-7

prayer

God, Your answers are perfect and I don't need to be afraid of them. Thank you for using the broken and healed areas in my life to bring hope and healing to others.

rooted in hope

questions

What obstacle to hope am I mired in? What stands between me and hope-filled waiting?

What steps can I take today to push through the enemy's boundaries designed to keep me stunted and weak?

Who can I be accountable to to grow in my faith as I abide in Him in this season?

scripture

Jeremiah 17: 7-8

prayer

God, I confess my own shortcomings, my own lack of hope in a season of waiting. Help me be satisfied with your timing. Help me dig down deep, seeking nourishment and Your anchoring.

how we hold our ground

questions

When has it seemed like God told me "No" but it turned out to be a bigger yes?

Where is God asking me to hold ground?

What does pushing through this look like right now?

scripture

Psalm 1:6, 2 Corinthians 4:17-18

prayer

God, I know You are trustworthy. I know You will show me everything I need to see as I trust You and obey.

shining through

questions

What breakthrough(s) have I been praying for?

How can I remember that God is so very near, regardless of what things look like?

What are some things He is asking of me in this season?

scripture

Isaiah 30:18, Psalm 34:7, 17-19, Romans 8:28

prayer

Dear God, what is the bigger vision that You have for me? Please give me a clearer picture of the calling You've placed on my life, and increase my faith and boldness to meet it.

waiting for home

questions

What is my go-to when deep life questions surface or when I feel confusing emotions?

Does this go-to draw me toward Jesus and into deeper relationship with Him?

In what ways do I feel "unqualified," and how can I surrender those fears of inadequacy to Jesus?

scripture

Psalm 42, Psalm 61:1-5, Psalm 139:1-18

prayer

Thank You, Father, that I can boldly come before you with all my thoughts and questions. I am safe to lay my heart bare before You – You know me completely, You never look down on me, and You give me the wisdom and assurance I seek.

budding

questions

How can I rest in small growth right now, and trust God for fullness?

What old, backburner prayer or dream have I shoved aside that God is prompting me to pick up again?

What is God telling me to do about it?

scripture

Ephesians 1:3-10, 2:8-10, Philippians 1:3-6

prayer

God, I haven't forgotten the things You've spoken to me about and placed in my heart, and I know You haven't forgotten them, either. Show me how to start praying and thinking about those things again, and show me what You want me to do about them.

what leads to victory

questions

What are some specific things I can do to nurture peace in my heart during this season? What things should I increase, and what things should I decrease? What new thing(s) should I add, and what old thing(s) should I eliminate completely?

How do I see God moving in my life currently?

scripture

Ephesians 3

prayer

Holy Spirit, show me how to start praying in color for the things You are speaking to me about. I am excited for Your answers and yielded to Your direction in my life.

notes

1. This story is found in 1 Kings 18.

2. Norman Grubb, *Rees Howells Intercessor* (Fort Washington, Penn: Christian Literature Crusade, 1980), 250.

3. Ibid, 228.

4. Ibid, 227.

5. Ibid, 230.

6. Shannon Guerra, *Oh My Soul* (Wasilla, Alaska: Copperlight Wood, 2018), 131.

7. This is from ABIDE *Volume 1: Rest in the Running*, in the chapter called "Upper Room People."

8. Genesis 1:1-2: *In the beginning, God created the heavens and the earth. The earth was without form and void, and darkness was over the face of the deep. And the Spirit of God was hovering over the face of the waters.*

also by shannon guerra

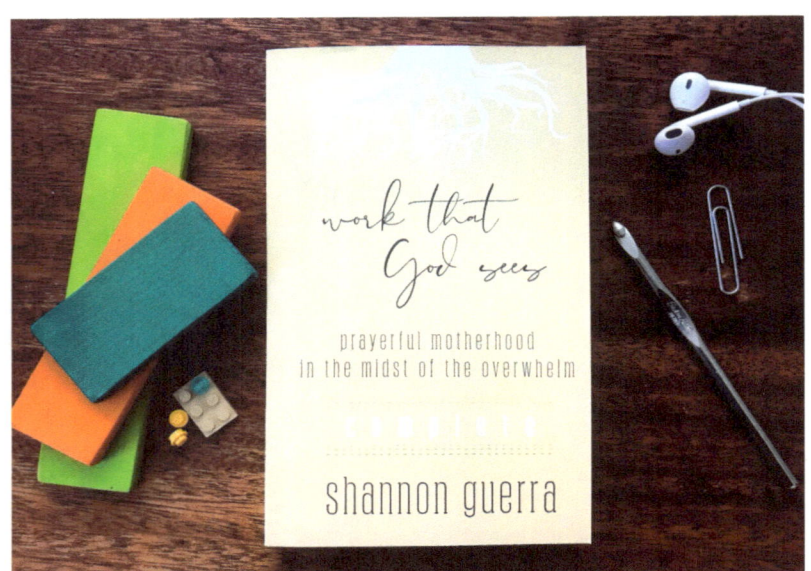 

the Work That God Sees series
prayerful motherhood in the midst of the overwhelm

Moms, you pour yourselves out every day. How about some powerful refilling, in small, easy doses?

Short chapters. White space. Deep down hope, and out loud laughter. Because you have what it takes. You are watched over and known by the God who notices every detail, and He meets you in these mundane moments and is breathing them into mighty movement.

Work That God Sees is available as six individual little books, or as a complete, all-in-one edition with the content from all six books (including the snarky recipes, crafty patterns, and questions for personal journaling or small group discussion) plus 25 pages of extra stories, recipes, and lessons you can learn at someone else's expense.

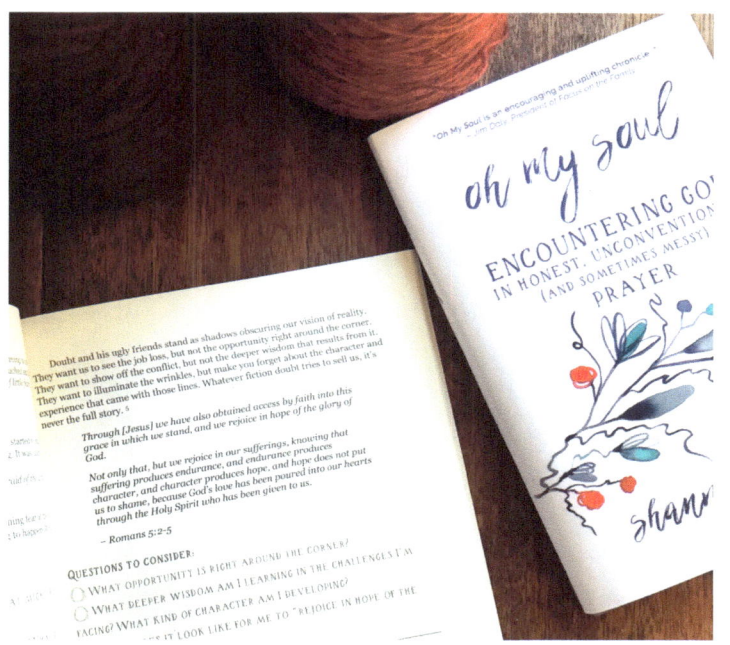

Oh My Soul

encountering God in honest, unconventional (and sometimes messy) prayer

What if there was **one thing** you could do that would always, without fail, make you more **whole** and **healed** and **at peace** than you were the day before...would you do it?

What if, at the same time, that one thing transformed the world around you?

This is what happens when we encounter God, living in His presence, in continual conversation with Him.

We want to hear God better, and to know His will for all the messy, mundane details of our life. But does He still speak to us when we are distracted, grumpy, overwhelmed, and unprepared?

How can we have "quiet time" with God when there's no quiet, and no time? Can we really know the will of God and move forward in obedience, in spite of our fears and failures?

And, if we're really honest with Him, will He strike us with lightning? Or will we end up praying with boldness and authenticity like never before?

Available as the original book, companion journal, and 21-day devotional study.

upside down

understanding and supporting attachment in adoptive and foster families

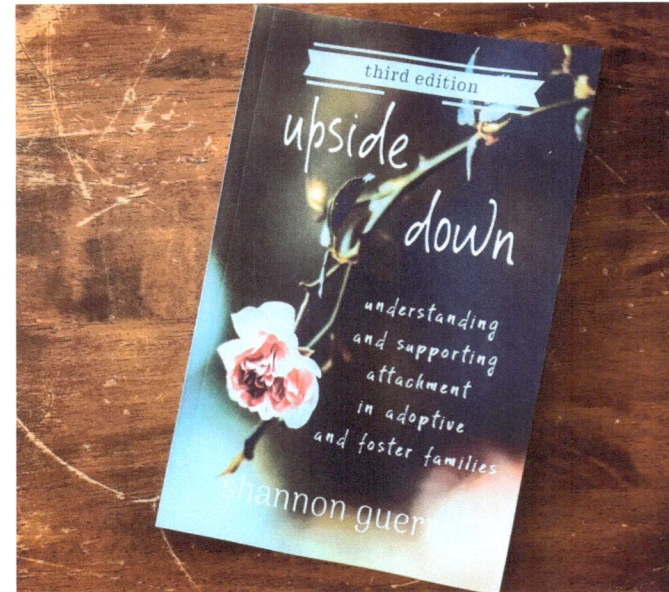

This book gives hope to adoptive and foster families, and the lowdown for those who love them.

Adoptive and foster families working through attachment issues often feel alone, but their communities can intentionally be part of the solution instead of unintentionally being part of the problem. Without that support, adoptive and foster families live in isolation.

Shannon Guerra learned this firsthand after she and her husband adopted two of their children in 2012. She started writing shockingly transparent blog posts about what her family was going through at home, at the doctor's office, and in her heart as a mama.

And then adoptive and foster families started writing back.

Their overwhelming, unanimous theme was, **"This is what I've wanted to tell people for so long. I wish everyone who knows our family could read this."**

This book is the result. In about 100 pages, *Upside Down* provides information and insight that transforms an outsider's assumptions into an insider's powerful perspective. Because adoptive and foster families should never feel alone, and our communities can be equipped to make sure they never feel that way again.

the ABIDE series

a year of growing deep + wide

volume titles:

rest in the running

hope in the waiting

clarity in the longing

bravery for the next step

obedience to move forward

surrendering to win

ABIDE is off the beaten path: A 6-volume series of fully illustrated books that are part devotional, part coffee table book, part magazine. These six beautiful books will lead you further into the presence of God as you grow deep and wide, pressing forward in these seasons that stretch us. Each book contains full color photographs, a light-yoked study section for personal or small group use, an extra recipe or two, and powerful encouragement that meets you where you're at and moves you forward.

one more thing...

Need a little white space in the chaos?

You are warmly invited to copperlightwood.com, where we're transparent about finding peace in the hard moments and beauty in the mess. I hope you'll hit the subscribe button and poke around all the posts and videos. Just keep in mind that it's a little unpolished here, so watch out for the Legos on the floor.

Bless you, friend,
Shannon Guerra

connect:
parler: shannonguerra
mewe: shannonguerra
gab: shannonguerra
clouthub: shannonguerra
facebook: copperlightwood
instagram: copperlightwood
goodreads: shannonguerra
pinterest: copperlightwood

email:
shannon@copperlightwood.com

www.ingramcontent.com/pod-product-compliance
Lightning Source LLC
Chambersburg PA
CBHW042257100526

44589CB00003B/52